Whispers of Spiritual Wisdom

Barbara M. Delong

Second Edition

ISBN: 978-1-989940-64-8
Dimensionfold Publishing
Dimensionfold.com

Table of Contents

Foreword 1
Introduction 3
Canyons of Crystal 7
Within 9
Memory's Whisper 11
In the Light 13
Call of Remembrance 15
Fertile Ground 17
Renewed 19
The Light Within 21
A Promise 23
The Calling 25
Heart Seeds 27
Flowers of Wisdom 29
Transcendence 31
The Answer 33
The Oath 35
Crystal Sight 37
The Pathway 39
Reborn 41
Time Now Near 43
The Key 45
Showing the Way 47
Eyes of the Soul 49
A New Rhyme 51
Balance Restored 53
Teardrops from Crystals 55
Blank Pages 57
A Memory Deep 59
Link with the Infinite 61
A Window in Your Soul 63
Cloaked in Rainbows 65
Love and Peace 67

Radiance...69

A Whisper Answered a Whisper 71

A Voice Never Used...73

The Light is You..75

Desert River...77

Cause and Effect...79

Reborn..81

Song of Your Soul 83

Ancient Wisdoms Call 85

The Pathway 87

Wisdom Within...89

Heart of Hearts...91

Meet the Future..93

In Harmony 95

Sweet and Sour 97

White Light..99

Dead End..101

On the Way to Eternity 103

Completed...105

New Meaning...107

Each Thought a Seed 109

Spiritual Stream 111

A Lifetime Past 113

After Thoughts...115

About The Author..117

Foreword

Letters represent sounds, groups of letters, which create words, represent thoughts, and strings of words form concepts. Turning those concepts into beautiful and relevant images is called magic. Barbara DeLong certainly does magic with words. With both poetry and dialogue, she stirs deeper thoughts that awaken higher levels of consciousness, conscience, spirituality, and hope. Barbara evades the limits of gravity, by lifting our reality above the physical and emotional and speaking to us on higher planes.

Cosmic, universal, and infinity are weighty words often thrown about carelessly. To Barbara, these heavy concepts are mere foundations and stepping stones leading up to an even greater reality. A dimension where the atmosphere is love, there are 50 ways to say give, but none for the concept of greed, and possibility has only one limitation, range of imagination. Having the pleasure of knowing her personally qualifies me to express a simple truth. She does not just express incredible things, she thinks them and lives them as well. To know Barbara, is to know love, generosity, patience, tolerance, imagination, optimism, and wonder. To not know Barbara, is to live in an acapella world.

- Patrick Cooke

Introduction

It is no secret that there is now a quickening in the cosmos, an awakening of spiritual energy within everyone. These are times of change and we feel it within, before we see it manifest within our realities. This is a time of seeking on all levels, looking for that spark of light that was instilled within us all, at the moment of creation. Because we are all unique, the manner in which we seek that light is as individual as the snowflakes that fall in the first winter storms, or the crystalline structures of individual grains of sand. It may seem as if everyone is going in different directions but the reality is all are seeking to find that spark of light and fan it into a flame to illuminate the spiritual understandings and philosophies that are carried within. There is a memory of it that urges us forward at this time, drawing us into the ultimate understanding that we are but one family, united by lights within that glow with ancient remembrances' of that unity, and the love that not only created us, but now draws us together once again.

Though the times we live in force us to focus on the physical reality for the sake of survival, now there is the added call of the spiritual, as this awakening energy becomes more and more intense within each of us. Some will look for sages and shamans, some will seek answers in religious texts, and others will seek out teachers, workshops, and courses of study. For the most part, the searching for the fuel for that inner spark is being sought on an external level. The reality is that the answers and wisdoms have always and still do rest within each of us.

There is an old story, passed down through the generations that tells of the time when humanity was created. The Gods created us after their image and instilled within us all of their powers and abilities. Realizing after the fact that they had also instilled within us immortality as well as the same powers of creation that they had. Not wanting to turn so powerful a race loose on the cosmos they decided to take those memories of the limitless energies that were within from us and hide them until we were ready to ascend into their ranks, The problem was where to hide them? One wise elderly sage said put that memory on the moon, but that was discarded because ultimately man would go there and most assuredly find those memories. Another suggested the bottom of the deepest sea, but that was eliminated for the same reason. The debate went on for eons until one of the wisest stepped forward and had the answer that all agreed to ... she said, "Hide that memory deep within their consciousness, they'll never think to look there." And so it was done.

We all carry within us the answers to all our questions as well as the philosophies for how to grow and evolve into the times we serve and function in. This is a time, when all will eventually learn of the magic that is carried within and how to use it with the same unconditional love that created us. As we seek, no matter how far we roam across the planet or into the cosmos, we will be called back to those inner, ancient memories of the connectedness of those lights within and how, when woven together with love, we create an energy more powerful than any on the physical plane. We are all seeking at this time the awakening of those philosophies and the manifesting of them through how we live our own personal lives. The spiritual is ever reaching channels to manifest within our physical realities and as we open those channels we begin to understand the limitless dimensions that can and will open to us.

Within this book are poems and short thoughts to ponder. It is my hope that they stir, within all, the remembrance of those areas that hold your own personal magic and that you listen to the spiritual whispers that you, yourself, have carried through time.

"We are not humans on a spiritual journey.
We are spiritual beings on a human journey."
Stephen Covey

Canyons of Crystal

Through canyons of crystal
Flow rivers of dreams
On currents of time
To dimensions unseen.

Unfold your wings of wishes
Let the winds of destiny guide you
Open your heart and welcome
The visions carried within.

For magic there awaits you
Harvested through time
Tis yours alone to awaken
You need only conjure the rhyme.

"Life is a mosaic of creation, and piece by piece we add to its grandeur.   The energies swirl around us and we find pieces of our lives in the most unusual of places. Often these pieces will complete parts of our realities we didn't know were incomplete. We gather, we sort, and we rearrange to expand that which we are. Piece by piece as the consciousness expands the vision to incorporate them all into that which we are. Every fragment of the puzzle or mosaic of our lives has import and relevance. To discard a piece is to become incomplete."

Within

Nature surrounds you and awaits your touch –
You blossom with spring –
And sing in harmony with the wind –
As you are one with nature –
So, too, are you one within.

The New Age is as Old as Time

"Every generation comes into the earth plane with the concept of a "new age" as they become aware of the immensity of the universe and our small place within it. As enlightenment or the understanding of the grander scheme occurs they welcome the dawning of a New Age. In reality the term and concept are as old as time its self. The term is used in the Bible and countless other ancient historical texts. As soon as humanity is able to understand that we are on a journey and are spiraling upwards towards new concepts and wisdoms they proclaim the "New Age" has arrived, and with each new generation there is once again a "new age" on the horizon."

Memory's Whisper

From another time –
A call long unanswered –
Demands to be heard –
And resolved.

A silent call upon memory's whisper –
A promise made, but not yet kept –
Returns again to await completion –
A challenge made that must be met.

Seeds of Wisdom

"There are countless individuals who have accumulated huge libraries and feel they have the knowledge of the universe at their fingertips. What they have are hundreds, perhaps thousands of books that hold ancient knowledge that served a time long past. Knowledge is only the beginning. "

"Accumulated knowledge represents seeds of wisdom that must be taken in, nurtured and absorbed into the consciousness and then manifested into the time they serve. If the seeds are not blended with the consciousness, then they are as ancient as the texts that held them, they serve no purpose or time."

"When the knowledge is used as the basis for the wisdom then and only then can it manifest and be of use to any time. We need to place our own personal experience and awareness alongside the knowledge of the past, to create the wisdom that will effectively serve the time in which we dwell."

In the Light

One who walks within the spirit –
Reaches out to your heart –
Friend and brother from time long past –
Now returns to help you grow –
Ever touching –
Sharing memories –
Opening doors that once were shut –
Bringing answers now to reason –
Now's the time for you to sow –
Guided ever by the spirit –
Friend and brother ever more.

Reach within and cast your seeds –
Loose them freely upon the light –
Touching now from past to present –
Taking with you what's gone before –

Ready now to make transition –
Open now to clearer sight –
As you travel life's long pathway –
Know your friend and spirit's there –
Ever watching, ever sharing –
One with you within the light.

"It is the journey that is the greatest teaching tool, not the final destination. Arriving anywhere is anticlimactic. The lessons, the difficulties and the hurdles are what add character and dimension to us. How we manage the trip, how we treat our fellow travelers and the manner in which we address the adversities that we encounter; are the true measure of what we have gathered and how well we have applied the universal laws and energies to our journey. The actual fact that we have arrived anywhere simply indicates that it is time for another trip or journey."

Call of Remembrance

Ancient echoes sound within your soul –
A call of remembrance, the realization of a goal –
The crystal light within your heart –
Casts rainbows and indicates the start –
Of a new direction – the dawn of a new day –
You listen within and find a new way.

"To get something you never had, you have to do something you never did. When the Infinite takes something from your grasp, He's not punishing you, but merely opening your hands to receive something better."

Fertile Ground

Ever weaving, ever growing –
Eternally seeking the light –
You open to wisdom –
Igniting inner sight.
The path is strewn –
With burdens let go –
You cross o'er the threshold –
And bask in the glow –
The seeds and the flame –
Converge all around –
You release what's inside –
You find fertile ground.
Touched by the breath –
Of the infinite source –
Your way is made clear –
Your soul sets its course.

"Energy is spoken of everywhere in the spiritual field. Healing energy, etheric energy, psychic energy and the list goes on and on. In my opinion there are really just two different kinds of energy that we deal with in this physical incarnation. There is the vital energy of the body, that energy that is generated as the physical body functions and provides the signals that trigger responses that we require for life. Then there is spiritual energy that comes directly from the other side, the spirit realms. This is channeled energy and not of this world or of the physical plane. It is limitless and flows from a source that is connected with creation itself. Spiritual energy, that which is channeled, is energizing, invigorating, it charges us and gives us a high that is not only legal but healing and limitless. Spiritual energy is channeled through the crown chakra and triggered by creative expression in the earth plane. We open the door with the creative process, creativity done just for the joy of creation."

Renewed

The gentle breezes brush your face
and whisper to your soul
Of times long past and times to come.
Of quests to be fulfilled.
The whispers echo, and then strike a chord
The light then dawns, the path is clear
The cycle's been renewed.

Are You a Parrot or a Prophet?

"For those of us in the spiritual fields and seeking enlightenment and wisdom there are at least two distinct pathways we can take; we can either be a parrot or a prophet. We read, we seek, we take classes, we study philosophy, but it's what we do with all that information that determines what role we play. There are many who pride themselves in all they have read and are able to quote chapter and verse of many ancient texts and the wisdoms of philosophers long since blended into the light. These are the parrots, ones who just repeat what others have learned and shared. Usually there is no independent thought just rote memory and the ability to bring forth someone else's wisdoms. Then there are the prophets; those who do all of the above, but instead of quoting ancient wisdoms they incorporate those wisdoms into their experiences of the current time frame, they blend the new with the old and bring forth an evolved version that speaks to the current time. These prophets build on the foundations laid down by past generations and evolve truth and wisdom adding their own to greatly enrich and expand into the future. Parrot is easy, while prophet requires that you put independent thought and inspiration into your philosophies. So which are you?"

The Light Within

A candle glows in the darkness
Fueled from the light within
Casting out doubt and fear
And establishing a beacon to light your way.
That which now is planted
Takes hold for all of eternity
And guides, not only you. but others as well.

It's not what life does to you, but rather what you do with
life that counts.

A Promise

Chimes in the wind call to your soul.
They awaken a dream from times long past.
Through time has it come.
To seek reality and fulfill a promise.

An echo within remembers that promise
The joy and elation pass through space
where there is no time
And once again two halves are joined
This time for all of eternity.

"There are those who call themselves teachers, who spout philosophies and wisdoms, and have not lived them or walked the talk. They speak empty words and empty wisdoms and will eventually be ignored. A teacher who has not experienced the lesson first hand has no right to try to teach the concept."

The Calling

As snowflakes drift upon the wind
And trust their fate unto the Infinite
So, too, do you drift for a time
And lead you on as they did before.
Allow the winds of time to keep you safe
To guide you home once more
To help you seek your heart's desire
And lead you on as they did before
For what you seek lies just beyond
And calls to you from deep within
You'll find it, hold it, and then let it go
For it will be part of you for all of eternity.

"Have you ever wished you had said something to someone and then not only the moment but the person had passed? It just isn't enough to tell them that their loved ones know they were loved, nor that they can feel the sentiments and don't really need the words. Those who are left behind do need the words and they need to know that their loved ones get the message. It becomes very important to let those who have passed over know how much they are loved and missed."

"Therapists will tell you to write letters and then not send them, or to burn them and let the smoke carry the message to those on the other side. It just doesn't seem to be enough. While doing platform medium ship I came to a woman who needed to really know her message was getting through. When I do this sort of communication the information I get is channeled from the spirit realms, often humorous, always wise. Her message from the spirit realms was to write a letter, address it to her loved one on the other side (mom, PO Box XOXOXO, Heaven), no return address, put a stamp on it and mail it. As I looked at this lovely woman who now had a confused look on her face, the rest of the message came through. When letters cannot be delivered, where do you think they go? You got it; The Dead Letter Office. Where do you suppose the dead go for their mail? It made perfect sense to me."

Heart Seeds

Upon your soul there rests a goal
A promise given long ago
A task was given to guide your soul
Seeds were shared for you to sow
Long have they rested within your heart
Carried within till the time was right
Now is the time to do your part
Now is the time, you have cleared your sight.
You open and balance, the focus is clear
They flow from your heart upon winds out of time
They find fertile soil in the joy of a tear
They open to spirit in rhythm and rhyme.

"Often it is hard to understand the meaning of our lives, the purpose of our being here and even more important, why lessons have occurred they way they did. When I was looking for a good way to explain this to a group I took a deep breath and asked for some clarification and the following is what came through."

"Each lifetime is like a huge jig saw puzzle. We gather pieces during our lifetimes and try to sort them out and fit them together into a cohesive whole. Each lesson we process provides us with another piece, often a pivotal one. We spend our lifetimes gathering pieces and finding usually by our thirties or forties that at least the outlines are complete, and we can sometimes gather a hint of where we are going and why we are here. There are always areas that defy interpretation but, given time they do clear up and often surprise us. By the time we make ready to go into the light there are only a few pieces remaining and with our passing, the puzzle is complete and we can view the picture that this lifetime created."

"Among the many lessons we gather each lifetime Patience is one that is eternally worked upon. Putting the pieces of your lifetime together required patience as well, often there is a piece missing in an aspect of your life, so you work on another area where you have more pieces. It's impossible to force pieces to fit where they do not belong. Patience is a cosmic quality gathered over time and generations of the soul's development."

Flowers of Wisdom

A seed is planted in fertile soil –
The seasons pass and sprouts it not –
A wanderer comes and pauses a while –
He shares his wisdom and then moves on.

The words fall as rain upon the seed -
Caress it, spark it and life reaches out –
Through fertile soil it bursts upon us –
A flower of wisdom, without a doubt.

For all to see, for all to share –
Each thought's a seed each word a prayer –
Each flower of truth holds wisdom dear –
When the time is right the way is clear.

"Unconditional is a word that is used a lot but not always, I fear, fully understood. It means without question, without strings, without conditions, no matter what. Qualities such as love, friendship, trust and faith all, for them to truly flourish, require the concept of being unconditional. Often we, being human, use the emotions as a bargaining chip and in so doing attach a string or condition on our friendship or love. When we do that we remove unconditional from the equation and reduce the meaning of our love or friendship. Love given unconditionally is the rarest gift of all, beyond riches. Striving for the unconditional aspects in life is one of the most noble of quests."

Transcendence

You reach to hold but cannot grasp
A point in time, a moment's peace
For all is movement, motion, seeking
Ever onward towards our goals
To release is to hold
To share is to own
To give is to multiply
To transcend is to make our dreams become our reality.

Healing doesn't come through prayer and promises - it comes to us through action and intent. How we live our lives in accordance with the golden rule? How we try to make sure our actions and intent do no harm to others? Our part in the healing process becomes harder but more challenging. We are works in progress. We have been given simple guidelines, if we choose to see them, and all it takes is walking the philosophy already deeply ingrained within our souls. Letting it out, applying it to everyone and everything, walking the light within and becoming the rule within opens us to infinite healing, love and wisdom.

We ask the Infinite to send us healing and restore balance to our lives - in order for that to happen we have to open the doors and pave the way through our actions and intent. The light flows strongly and positively along those channels that are open to it, and willing to open to the illumination that comes with it. Those who so choose become beacons of light, living examples that radiate the wisdom and joy that comes from following that seed of radiance implanted within by the Infinite. This means that others who are not so fortunate, who are still seeking within get the benefit and the overflow of the healing energy and take in that energy to help open them to that which they carry within as well. The light acts as a magnet, attracting those who carry it and don't know it - healing is achieved by proxy.

The Answer

Wisdom from within
Provides the answer
For the question without.

When man was created by the Infinite Spirit, one of the gifts given which was not given other creatures was that of free will. Over the generations of evolution, over thousands of years, we often treat this gift lightly, not realizing the richness it provides us nor the price we pay. You see, it really isn't free. Yes, we have the freedom to make choices that often are not those that a caring parent would recommend, and often we wander far from the pathway that the spirit within is trying to guide us towards. We choose how we journey and whom we journey with whether or not it is good for us. We can choose to take side pathways and to follow dead ends, or to not even journey at all within a lifetime, all along exercising our right to free will. However, there is a price we pay. Along with free will we must accept as well the consequences of those choices and alterations we freely exercise. The problem is, often we complain about our situations and circumstances, without claiming the responsibility for them as well.

I found myself looking at many situations that were not exactly comfortable and complaining to the universe. When I stopped muttering for a time to catch my breath a very soft whisper reminded me that they were the result of choices that I had made with my "free will". That's when I got very quiet and started to look around to see if anyone had been listening to my complaining, aside from the universe. On careful and embarrassing reflection I have started to rework some of my choices and amazingly, things have started to clear up and move once more.

The Oath

Chimes in the wind call to your soul –
They awaken a dream from times long ago –
Through the years has it come –
To seek reality and fulfill a promise –
An echo within remembers the oath –
The joy and elation pass through space
where there is no measure –
This time for all of eternity.

"How we reflect upon others and how others perceive us is a prime consideration in our lives. Reflection is a most important quality within all of us, for it shows us who we are and what we want to be. Each of us has countless reflections and they are seen differently by all we come into contact with. Often what we see with our physical eyes is not the reality of what we are projecting. There is always a time of inner reflection; a time of coming into harmony with the reality of who we are and the purity of spirit that is carried within. Opening ourselves to who we really are, without the cloaks of what we think others are expecting of us is to reflect the light within and allows the spirit to take form within this reality. We are, after all, a reflection of our inner purpose and direction, of our connection with creation. To mask that is to deny our own divinity."

Crystal Sight

A barrier crossed – a burden lifted –
You rise above – and see the light –
It shines through you – a soul most gifted –
It brings you peace – and crystal sight.

"Wisdom is brought from out of time, stored within for generations of the soul's evolution. Wisdoms are gathered lifetime after lifetime, like the pieces of a gigantic puzzle to be reassembled only when all of the pieces had been gathered. Through a lifetime the puzzle is brought back to wholeness and new insights and levels and dimensions of wisdom are brought forward into the consciousness of mankind. Eons ago, before recorded time humanity embraced these wisdoms and used them wisely for the healing and abundance of all. And then there was a time of darkness when the magic and miracles were lost to the memories and stored within until it was time to open those doors once more and to use those skills and understandings to restore the peace within the human heart and consciousness. The emergence of those wisdoms and their incorporation into reality will start slowly. Those who first draw upon them and remember their power will help others to do the same. It will take time but as there is the dawning of the memories once again. There is ascension of consciousness and new pathways will be found that bring true magic into the realms of everyday life."

The Pathway

A quiet comes from out of time –
It lifts you, frees you and lets you see –
That which you sought, that which you held –
Was released in love and has set you free.
To walk the pathway, lit by love –
Protected by faith and guided by light.

"Energies are constantly swirling and bringing back to us reflections of the energies that we have been sending out into the universes. Pay close attention to all that transpires in your life, for it will truly tell you whether or not your energetic broadcasts are tuned to the right channel or not. Often we make the mistake of assuming that what we think on occasion is the energy we are sending out into the universe. It is our intent, character, actions and consciousness that determine what comes back at us. In order for the law of attraction to truly work we must walk the path we want to draw to us. If love is desired then love must be given unconditionally, If richness is sought, then it must be given freely without expectations of reward. That which you seek on a heart level must be radiated out and given to everyone you touch. This is a law of investment and only when you have invested enough does it start to flow back at you."

"If you are not happy with the people you are attracting, change yourself. If life is not sending you what you think you deserve, change your approach to life and put a bit more spirituality into it. A cosmic mirror is being held up to all of humanity, from a personal to a global level. Pay attention, it will tell you a lot about yourself and the times in which we live. Better yet, we all still have a chance to change for the better."

Reborn

Out of time are you called by a memory rich –
It reaches within and sounds a chime –
That rings throughout eternity.

A call to remembrance, a call to wisdom –
Of secrets guarded and memories shared –
Of goals now met and purpose renewed.

You are charged once more to carry the flame –
To light the way and guard the light –
For those who follow, for those who seek –
Reborn, renewed, you meet the challenge and set the pace.

"Finding strength in new areas of life is a quest we should always pursue. This will give you power to find the courage to confront issues in life that we have been hesitant to touch. In many ways the sleepers are awakened and there is a new strength where in the past there has been none. From deep within, hidden from sight there has lurked strength and compassion, courage and conviction. Individuals find that where once they were timid and withdrawn, now they step forward and are counted. This applies to the entire population and crusaders are reborn into a new time, but with a familiar cause; to right wrongs on all levels."

Time Now Near

Crystal dew drops from dawns early past –
Create within you a pull to return –
To a place out of time, out of reason –
For there will be found what you seek –
To return once again, the pathway now clear –
Out of time – into time – for all time –
From the past to the future –
The time is now near.

"Most of us are familiar with trinities of all sorts, we have grown up with them and they flow from our tongues easily. For those who are on the spiritual pathway there is another to add to the list that is of great import."

"We are creations of the Infinite and as such we provide a link in the spiritual DNA of the universe. It was the creative energy and unconditional love of the Infinite that evolved us into creation. Creative energy is the fuel of all that is. By manifesting creative energy we send a signal to the universe that we understand this process and are willing to fuel this lifetime with that creative energy. Manifesting creative energy within our lives sets in motion the spiritual flow of wisdom that in turn moves our physical lives along out pathways."

"When life seems as if it isn't moving along fast enough for you look for what you are doing on a creative level, just for the sheer joy of creating. Chances are that life has gotten in the way of the creative process and those things that gave you joy on the creative levels have been put aside. You fuel your life with the creative energies, when they are absent; things come to a grinding halt. By getting creative you add richness to your life, the spiritual will once again flow into your energy field and life will move ahead."

"A word of insight … the creative process needs to be done on a regular basis; one day just won't cut it. The creative energies can manifest in all sorts of different ways, be creative about being creative and you greatly increase the abundance it can bring into your life."

The Key

A call from within you –
Leads to a timeless discovery of purity –
You carry within you the key to the answer –
Of a question never asked.

You pass through a doorway to a place not remembered –
And open to knowledge that is yours for all time –
You feed the hunger that calls out to be quenched –
And seek out the pathway – now lit by the glow from
within.

"There is great power in the spoken word, far more than could be imagined. Once words are spoken they take on lives of their own; the more we repeat ourselves the greater the power we put into them. The universe eventually will not be able to tell the difference between a spoken thought and actual reality and will compel us to actually manifest those words. We think aloud, promising to create a project, realize a dream or climb an emotional mountain. The imprint of those words upon the element of time creates a contract with the universe and we unwittingly commit to the manifestation of our own words; they represent a promise to the spirit within and the universe embraces it as well, creating a flow of energy that directs us towards the fulfillment of that promise. This often results in life taking on directions that we don't expect and in some cases are not very comfortable with."

"The old saying, "be careful what you ask for", evolved from the reality that when you put it out there the universe goes into action and helps you to realize your request. The more you cooperate with the universe once this takes place the easier life can be. Your words make the commitment, they reinforce that commitment and by doing so you put energy into the realization of that thought. For those on a spiritual pathway this is greatly increased. Take care with what you put out there; make sure you are going to take action and are willing to work for what your words commit you to."

Showing the Way

Darkness cloaks a special glow –
And protects it from the storm –
You shelter a spark –
And bring it home –
In your light darkness yields –
And lights unite –
Showing the way for the multitudes.

"We are surrounded by blessings, by miracles every day, by small ones and big ones. Most of the time, we don't recognize, or even acknowledge them. When times get difficult we are even less inclined to notice the small blessings that are showered down upon us every day. I'm just as guilty as anyone of ignoring them and when I do, life tends to get a bit bleak. Of course all of us want a full fledged miracle, something that defies science and reason, to happen in our lives; something that would make the six o'clock news. But would we really recognize one, if it hit us in the face? I wonder what if I was on the other side of the equation so to speak. Not the one begging for the miracles but rather the one supplying them. How would I feel if none of the millions of small miracles I had supplied were enough, or appreciated, or even acknowledged? Would I be inclined to shower huge gifts on humanity if the small ones were taken for granted and not considered enough? I think we're very lucky that the Infinite Spirit has unconditional love for us, and continues to give in spite of the fact that as a whole we seem to be not to appreciative for all of the blessings that are showered upon us every day."

"There is an old song called Count Your Blessings and it holds great wisdom. It tells us to count our blessings, count them one by one, count our many blessings see what God has done. It goes on to say that when you're down or sad that counting your blessings relieves sadness and brings light into your life … and it does."

Eyes of the Soul

The seas of time wash against the shores of eternity –
Your path is clear –
To walk in the light and glimpse that which is to come –
To share the joy in the true knowledge –
The infinite is within all equally –
Your eyes, the eyes of your soul –
Will share in the peace –
Of the love of tomorrow.

Druids, Wizards and Fairies
"From The Leaves of Light"

Through canyons of crystal
Flow Rivers of dreams
On currents of time
To dimensions unseen.

Unfold your wings of wishes
Let the winds of destiny guide you
Open your heart and welcome
The visions carried within.

For magic there awaits you
Harvested through time
Tis yours alone to awaken
You need only conjure the rhyme.

A New Rhyme

The wind carries memories from out of the past –
That ripples upon the mirror of your soul –
Causing you to awaken to a time that comes again –
A message within a message to reach a goal.

Within your memories there rests a key –
To open a store house whose message now calls –
You reach for the key and discover within –
A new side of you full of richness and peace.

There emerges an awareness, it manifests in reality –
Your direction is changed, your perception refined –
A new level of vibration, an increase of intensity –
You are baptized in light –
Reborn in crystal purity –
Awakened to a new rhyme of the universe.

The Golden Rule
The Dove and Olive Branch of Peace

The Golden Rule, we've all heard it. Most of us have quoted it to death. It's so well known you just have to say "the Golden Rule" and almost everyone knows what you're talking about. I knew that it came from the Bible and was one of the quotes attributed to Jesus. That is true, but that isn't the original source, the philosophy has been around since before the beginning of recorded history. This thread of wisdom has woven its way throughout time and history becoming a part of every religion and philosophy we have. It is found it in most of the Philosophies and Religions through time:

570 AD - Islam - "Not one of you truly believes until you wish for others what you wish for yourself" - written by the prophet Muhammad.

6TH century BC - Shinto - "Do not do to others what you do not want done to yourself"

2,000 years ago - Christianity - "In everything, do to others as you would have them do to you; for this is the law and the prophets."

2,500 years ago - Buddhism - "Treat not others in ways that you yourself would find hurtful."

5TH century BC - Taoism - "Regard your neighbor's gain as your own and your neighbors loss as your own".

1,800 years BC - Judaism - "What is hateful to you, do not do to your neighbor. This is the whole Torah; all the rest is commentary."

Balance Restored

Lost, yet ever present –
A treasure of no value –
You have only to let go to hold.

When whispers become loud enough –
Questions will be answered –
The air cleared –
And balance restored.

For every effect there is a cause –
For every tear shed, laughter –
For every loss, a gain –
We have only to be open –
And ready to experience.

"Cosmically speaking this is a time of great transition, the energies are shifting, climates going crazy, and there is social unrest in the most unexpected of areas. The first decade of the 21st Century may well go down in history as one of the most unsettled times in quite a while, at the same time it is exciting because of all the changes going on within the consciousness of humanity. And change is happening."

"Those who had slumbered along, trusting that their needs would be taken care of are waking up to the fact that, while they slumbered, others plundered. People are starting to take responsibility for their own well being and standing up for what they believe in, they're own inner truths. Where once there were hoards of lemming like masses blindly following leaders that convinced them they knew best; now there are questions everywhere and the truth is rooted out no matter how cleverly is had been disguised."

"This is a time for truth and change and the universal energies are fueling the consciousness of all of humanity. As great numbers find that the security they once had is now gone, they are finding strength and passion for new endeavors that allow them to explore new horizons. The spirit of the explorer, of one who breaks new ground and inspires the young is alive and well within the hearts and minds of many. The old structure no longer provides the support for the truth of the future so it will be shifted and expanded according to the dreams of the founders but evolved into the time it must serve."

Teardrops from Crystals

Teardrops formed from crystals –
Rest upon the garden deep –
They merge with seeds long planted –
They spark them into life.

The garden blooms with life's true cause –
The crystals light the way –
As truth and love and wisdom spread –
Mankind blossoms into a new day.

Tomorrow touches yesterday –
A cycle begins once more –
And teardrops, formed from crystals –
Filled with light, begin the new day.

"There are many gardens that each of us are responsible for within this lifetime. There are the spiritual gardens within, wherein we tenderly work with growing new truths and beliefs that apply to this lifetime. We nurture those concepts that are just starting to emerge and we protect them from all manner of threat. We feed and water, so that they can grow and be added to the arsenal of creative tools that helps us to manifest love and harmony within our realities. There are no weeds in our spiritual gardens, for whatever grows there was planted by us in lifetimes past to grow and mature at just the right time. The spiritual gardens are a wonderful sanctuary for our spirits, for not only do truths grow there but also peace, wholeness, creativity, and healing. There is a harmony of spirit here and fantasy and reality blend for a magical wondrous inner realm."

"Then there are the conscious gardens where thoughts and dreams are scattered and nurtured as best we can. This garden is a bit unorganized for our attention is easily drawn from one area to another and often we do not balance that attention. Conscious gardens often do not have the flow and beauty that the etheric ones do but they can be abundant and pretty in their own wild way. Weeds here can be distracting but often random thoughts are the answers we seek so don't pull any. You never know what the flower will be like unless you give it time to bloom … The same wisdom can be applied trees that bear fruit. Everything should be given the chance to mature and prove its worth; for everything has worth if we give it a chance."

Blank Pages

The past is a book whose pages are filled –
The future is blank pages –
You are the author –
You determine story line and outcome –
Your pen is far from out of ink –
As each chapter closes there is within –
The seed for that which is to come.

"There is also the garden of family and friends. This is a most unique one for if you compare them to flowers you will find there is direct correlation. Some will be beautiful and exotic; some will have great fragrance and some thorns, and yet all have purpose within your lives. Though you can't always figure out why some are in your garden please remember that they are there for a purpose (not to annoy you). Reflect on the fact that some of the strangest and unattractive plants have amazing healing qualities and serve mankind well."

A Memory Deep

A ray of light found its way –
To my door from far away –
Entwined with joy, with laughter flowing –
My soul set free, once more is glowing –
This light so free and pure of thought –
Reminded me of what was taught –
So long ago in lifetimes past –
Renewed today, once more to cast –
A memory deep upon my heart –
To join once more, restore a part –
That drifted long on winds of time –
Returns to me and completes what is mine –
A timeless love reborn and whole –
Once more complete, you share my soul.

"The element of new birth is always in our future, as old structures are vacated and old thought patterns released. We are constantly moving into phoenix rising energy, where everything is reborn out of the ashes of the old. This will always be a time of renewal on many levels as we move into an era of new thought and focus. Old methods, though familiar, no longer work, so new ones are brought in to expand awareness and give us a greater vision of what the future holds for us. The roles we play, are for a time comfortable, but eventually no longer hold our potential, so we change and expose facets of our characters that were held within for a very long time. We then display a greater depth of character and personality that was not before revealed."

"Some step out of the shadows where they have been content in the past to dwell, and move into the spot light where they have belonged all the time. Many will come of age in these times of change and will unveil qualities that were always present yet have gone unrecognized. There will be depth of character and qualities of wisdom that come from out of left field, and most will surprise themselves. There will be those who had been content with their lives and situations that now find themselves following new careers and manifesting new talents. It is a time of emergence, but for that to happen, much must change and there are those who do not like change, who will fight it in their lives."

Link with the Infinite

The temple within, wherein dwells your link with the
infinite –
Stands against all that would sway you. Know that always
–

You may rest there and be safe, to nurture yourself –
For what you will meet along the way.

"All will, in their own way, reflect on the love and loves within their lives. This is a most important element within our spirits for universal love is the fuel of all of creation. It was within this energy that all souls were created and then scattered throughout the cosmos to begin journeys that will one day return us to the source, the creator. Each of us has within us a spark, an infinitesimal speck of the creator and the universal, unconditional love that created us. Deep within the souls memory there rests a remembrance of that moment of unconditional love in which the spark of the creator was bestowed upon us. It is the echo of that love through time that has, and will continue to act as a compass, guiding us through lifetime after lifetime towards our journeys end, gathering along the way experiences of unconditional love, that fuel the inner specks and fan them into a flame of understanding and compassion for all of humanity."

"There is a new time upon us, an age of spirit, one in which we become co creators of our universe and reality. When we were blinked into creation there was a link that was formed between us and the source of our creation. This lifetime we have the opportunity to add a link to the chain of creation through our own creative energies and the unconditional love within us. We ascend to a level of consciousness where we are capable of the element of unconditional love and therefore worthy of adding to that chain. We have spent lifetimes searching for and gathering aspects of unconditional love from life's many different levels.

A Window in Your Soul

There is a whisper that drifts upon the wind –
It reaches you and touches your soul –
A seed, a spark, unite –
And abundance is yours –
Because a whisper answered a whisper.

A window in your soul –
Opens to the whisper of another –
Shadows are erased –
And peace is restored –
Awareness and acceptance –
Allow hurt to finally heal.

"When babies enter into this world they carry within a fully developed soul energy that is aware and fully present. It is a soul energy that has full access to the complete spectrum of the soul's development. In other words, way more evolved than any of us. The only problem is that the baby isn't able to articulate any of this wonderful information to us. We must seem pretty silly talking baby talk and cooing over this fully evolved spirit; and so they laugh at us, they throw back their heads and laugh. We think it's our behavior, and in a way it is, but really they are laughing at our total lack of understanding of the situation."

"As babies grow, their personalities and ego's for this lifetime come to the fore and the spirit energy, with all that wonderful information slips into the recesses of the consciousness so that the lessons for this lifetime can be experienced and whatever experiences that are needed can be gathered for the further development of the soul carried within. The soul has to work through the ego and the personality selected for this lifetime and learns all over again; to bring the inner wisdom into the consciousness by reminding itself through experience."

"So the next time you get to hold a very young child look into those eyes that will reflect back to you a fully evolved spirit with total awareness. This is a good time to impart your wisdoms to the spirit within. Speak not as one who is informed but rather one who is seeking; and if you get laughter you know your journey has amused the spirit within."

Cloaked in Rainbows

Remembrance of times past –
Awakens a yearning within –
You reach for understanding –
And grasp reality –
Cloaked in rainbows –
And completing a cycle –
A step forward into the light.

"You find yourself drawn to the past. Revisiting in your memories, ones who are no longer here and times that have changed greatly. The past holds warm smiles for you and there is always a feeling of a need to reconnect with those who you have lost contact with. A good idea for it grounds you and gives you a better feeling of where you came from. You revisit old homes and places where you grew up, in memory if not in reality. You recapture the feeling of youth and its infinite possibilities. This reawakens within you some of the dreams that had been put aside as you grew. They are still there and still awaiting your efforts to make them happen. Nothing is impossible, there is always a way if you but seek it with creative imagination. After all even adults play and make believe from time to time. It takes us back to the wonders of childhood and brings healing laughter into our energies."

Love and Peace

The song of your soul croons to humanity –
The whispers echo and magnify –
That which you keep hidden –
Comes to the light and creates rainbows –
To reflect on the surface of your soul –
And reach deep within to universal love and peace.

"How we relate with others is directly related to how we relate with ourselves. So if there are external conflicts then look within and check out the origin inside. It is never to soon to get to know yourself again and then apply the growth that has taken place within to how you relate to the outside world. This can be fun, it doesn't have to be work, and you choose how you want to approach it. Eventually, you should be surrounded by laughter because of the changes you've made. They don't feel major but just subtle alterations that make a world of difference not only to you but to those closest to you as well."

Radiance

When your light shines the brightest –
It comes from within –
And you will bask in its radiance –
As will those around you.

"Dreams to give us insight into the future; the problem is that they are symbolic and we have to figure out what the symbolism is in order to understand what the unconsciousness is trying to tell us. Rest assured it is always of a positive nature no matter what the dream is. Sometimes dreams are strange to get our attention that change is coming. If you so choose to journal, know that each has their own time frame in which the dream manifests its message.   Once you figure out yours, whether it be six weeks or six days, it gives you an edge on others to a degree in that you know when to expect change or an alteration in the flow of energy around you. This is a time when there is a new vibrancy around each of you and how you use that vibrancy will determine the insight you gather that can be put to good use in your reality, and thusly enriching you on many unusual and exciting levels."

A Whisper Answered a Whisper

There is a whisper that drifts upon the wind -
It reaches you and touches your soul.
A seed, a spark, unite -
And abundance is yours -
Because a whisper answered a whisper.
A window in your soul -
Opens to the whisper of another.
Shadows are erased -
And peace is restored.
Awareness and acceptance -
Allow hurt to finally heal.

"Universal energies draw us closer together. We are drawn towards understanding, each on their own level of consciousness, to the ones that we represent, while gathering wisdom and weaving it into the fabric of our very souls. All have hidden talents, or gifts, brought forth from lifetimes past. They choose their own moments in an evolution to present themselves and if we give them the channels to manifest, they can greatly enrich the experience we encounter. Just because you never painted, or wrote, doesn't mean you can't, it just means you haven't yet. Remember, that if something gives you joy it doesn't matter what others think, (as long as it isn't illegal). The universe is flowing with creativity, so each will find there are new and even interesting ways to use this energy. If, you decide to join the flow, you will not regret it, for it brings joy and ebullience into your life that will become a part of your reality, and give you laughter in places you never expected."

A Voice Never Used

A doorway appears from a solid wall –
The latch opens inward, triggered by a call –
From a voice never used, yet clear as a chime –
From a well deep within –
Summoned from beyond time.

"There are many lessons to be gathered through our lives that bring great wisdom to our lives. If we take the counsel that these lessons bring us, life will get more abundant and joyful. If we turn away from the lessons they will come again, but not as gently as they do at first."

The Light is You

Let not the past cloud the future.
What has been let go need not be regained,
For growth has changed your needs.
There will be, when the time is right,
An open door, a bright new light.
There is honor and dignity, wisdom and courage,
Surrounded by laughter and love.
The light is within you.
The light is you.

"We are entering a time of signs, a time when the universe gives each of us the sign we have asked for, but not necessarily in the manner we expect. Brace yourself, for the universe does give us what we ask for, but not always in the manner we would expect. These signs are often subtle but they will be there, so be alert. Watch for the unusual in the usual places; things happening out of sequence, or questions answered before the question was articulated. Don't look for the burning bush or claps of thunder; the universe has been there, and done that."

Desert River

A candle glows in the darkness
Never to go out.
The light created
Casts out shadows and spreads love.
A bridge appears where there was none
A river in the desert
You reach out and grasp a hand
A bond formed
Never to be broken.

"The etheric breezes bring us understanding beyond reason. This does not apply to the lottery or horse races, but to other, deeper qualities within the human spirit. Try to feel more in tune with the rhythm of our lives and the purpose of those around us. Try not to use this gift, for it is more enlightening when it comes of its own accord. There will be vivid dreams and premonitions that will all have positive reflections on our futures. Remember that most of the information is symbolic. It is good to keep notes or a journal for a lot of the imagery becomes clear only with the passage of time. Use it, and it can only bring you greater abundance in the future."

Cause and Effect

Lost, yet ever present
A treasure of no value
You have only to let go to retain.
When whispers become loud enough
Questions will be answered
The air cleared
And balance restored.
For every effect there is a cause
For every tear shed - laughter
For every loss - a gain
We have only to be open
And ready to experience.

"The energy of change and transition are all around you. Listen to the quiet message from the universal energies and bring that change into every aspect of your reality. Change is good; it awakens new aspects and dimensions not seen before. You need not make the changes radical, but the more change there is the greater the new light you bring into your life and reality, and the greater the potential you open to yourself. There is a time to let go of those aspects that do not enrich you on some levels and make room for greater outlets for your creative talents and greater potential for the gifts you carry within. For some, there has been a feeling that something must be changed and they look for the channels. For others the way is clear and you only need to take the first step to be swept away with the creative flow just waiting for your call. Which ever way you flow, know that change can only open new magic to your life. It is your choice and free will as to how much you wish to allow to flow into your reality."

Reborn

A ray of sun light found its way -
To my door from far away -
Entwined with joy, with laughter flowing -
My soul set free, once more is growing -
This light so free and pure of thought -
Reminded me of what was taught -
So long ago in lifetimes past -
Renewed today, once more to cast -
A memory deep upon my heart -
To join once more, restore a part -
That drifted long, on winds of time -
Returns to me, and completes what is mine -
A timeless love, Reborn and whole -
Once more complete, you share my soul.

"Universal energies swirl around you bringing you memories of the ancestors past and those who are still with you. This is a time of pulling together those memories. Old pictures and gatherings will awaken memories and stories of the past. Record them, remember them, and embrace the love and laughter they awaken within you. The ancestors gifted you each with much wisdom and great lessons. Reach back and find them and bring those wisdoms and gifts into this reality. The courage and strength it took in the first place is also a part of your heritage. For those who have no records or memories, times of quiet thought and meditation will awaken within you memories of lifetimes past, which also bring the wisdom and gifts into your realities. This is a time to honor those who brought you to this point in time; gathering with those who are still here is a wonderful way to start, but not the only way. The act of silently honoring those who in many cases are nameless works just as well and the thought is as good as the deed."

Song of Your Soul

The song of your soul croons to humanity -
The whispers echo and magnify -
That which you kept hidden -
Comes to the light, and creates rainbows -
To reflect on the surface of your soul -
And reach deep within to universal love and peace.

"There is always a need to search out and find a teacher, a guide, one who will direct you to the inner enlightenment that at times seems to elude your reach and grasp. Some will feel frustrated in not finding the source they seek, while others will just get on with their lives and ignore the inner pulling. It is a time of inner seeking, not outer seeking. That which is calling you is within, and you need only silence your inner chatter to find it. This requires you to seek out silence and quiet. We need to set aside a time each day to listen to the inner silence which holds all the answers you seek. Not in words but in philosophy that will lead you to the inner discovery you seek. Teachers are fine for the ABC's, but when it comes to inner enlightenment, the teacher is within and all you need to do is quiet your mind and you will find that wisdom you seek. How will you know it when you find it? Simple – it will not tell you what to do but rather give you're the light and tools to find it yourself. No real teacher ever answers a question, but rather asks another that sends you on a quest for knowledge. If you are given the answer, you'll stop looking and learning."

Ancient Wisdoms Call

A dream speaks to an inner need
A door is opened you thought sealed tight
A gift of love becomes a seed
That sheds the light for crystal sight.
You quest for truth and find much more
The inner whispers point the way
The soul begins to soar
As spirits awaken to share the day.
You hold the key to much long past
Those ancient wisdoms call to you
Your way is clear, the die is cast
You bridge the space from old to new.

"There comes a time in life to shift things around and create a new energy in all aspects of your life. Shake off the structures that have restricted you and free yourself from boundaries that now seem to not fit. This is a normal process and happens at different times in everyone's lives. Stretch your wings and fly. Allow yourself to live your dreams and become them. Why not? Letting go of structures and forms that no longer fit isn't always easy but once accomplished it is freeing and opens you to greater visions than one could have ever imagined. Recreating yourself is a most exciting prospect, and this is just the beginning; it does take long for the process to be completed. That first step is a big one, but the rest flow easily and you'll wonder what took you so long at some point in time."

The Pathway

A whisper comes from out of time.
It lifts you, frees you, and lets you see
That which you sought
That which you held
Is released in love and sets you free.
Ahead lays the pathway you must explore.
Protected by faith and guided by light.
You seek the way of your soul's true destiny
And attune yourself to the crystal sight.

"There is a feeling of gathering in the universal energies in the cosmic atmosphere. Many feel as if they need to stock up on material objects and others will be gathering new wisdoms and books to nurture and enlighten them. It is a time to take stock and fill those areas that seem wanting within your lives. Often we have neglected aspects of our lives in lieu of the more important physical realities needs. It is a time to address those areas that were softly and silently moved to make room or the minor disasters of the day. Time to balance out your life and pay attention to the creative projects ignored"

"In order to be in balance we need creative energies in equal measure to others that "seem" more important. The creative mellow out moments and supply new and unique vision, if we but bring it into our lives. So gather it in and allow it to provide you with new directions and vaster vistas to explore."

Wisdom Within

The mists will clear -
Your path will open before you.
Where you questioned, the answers will come -
Where choices were many,
Now only one.
Remember the voice -
That speaks to you only.
The wisdom within -
Will guide you -
Will light your way -
And lead you through Tomorrow.

"New wisdoms cascade around everyone, the elements of growth and learning are in the air and most are drawn to the books in one way or another. The written word opens doors to understanding and the opportunity to expand the potential that is within. The inner wisdoms ca be drawn forth and applied to reality. Draw upon what has been stored within from this and lifetimes past, and apply it to the here and now. Being sent back to the books is a way of awakening memories of what has been learned but not yet applied to life. Often we "know" the correct course of action; we just don't act upon the internal wisdom. Take time for action and application, and take the opportunity to stretch the intellect, to draw it into new realms of exploration. The element of learning takes on new meaning as many are drawn into lessons not connected to formal school, yet crucial to the evolution of the spirit. Lessons of all sorts will be recognized and applied to life and there will be a greater richness on all levels for those who gather the lessons and apply them to their lives."

Heart of Hearts

To give of one's self is a great gift indeed.
To give of the Infinite through one's self is greater still.
That is within you,
You will share with many,
And be doubly blessed within your heart of hearts.

"A strong, yet subtle universal image is that of a flickering flame. The energy lightens and then dims as we quest for answers to questions held deeply within. Energy for this week will ebb and flow as a candle flame flickers in a soft breeze. Go easy on yourselves for your energy as well will ebb and then flow. Take time for inner reflection and relaxation no matter how busy you are. The light will dawn on many of those areas that you have been looking for insight on. Often answers seem to come and go ... too quickly to grasp and hold. Have patience with yourself for in time they solidify and become understandable. Flickering flames may not give off great heat, but they do cast much light and dispel shadows within the human spirit. The flicker is for more than just atmosphere, it gives us time to get clarity of vision and insight into deeper meanings to initial fight."

Meet the Future

When tears cease and the laughter reigns
Wisdom surrounds you
And with love you move
Forward to meet the future.

"Change is perpetually in the air, and growth on all levels in all areas is rich within the energies. It is a time for moving to new levels of understanding within the human element. It is a time when we move into greater awareness of the energies that ever surround us. A greater acceptance of the spiritual natures of all around us is available to those who are ready to embrace it. A time of ascension of awareness, a time when part of the veil between levels of awareness shifts and we are given a greater understanding of the wisdoms that ever guide us within our reality. It is a time of initiation, a time when we are given the light to reach within our own personal shadows and understand the purpose of much within our lives. Spiritual and practical awareness is shared at this time and for those who have actively been seeking there is indeed a reward, a light at the end of the tunnel so to speak. For those who have not been actively stretching themselves there is also reward, though not quite as profound as the other. They will have ah-ha moments, times when reason comes suddenly to chaos. This is a time of light and wisdom, how much depends on where you are within this lifetime."

In Harmony

Always within reach, yet never held
Soaring within your soul
Awaiting the call to awareness.
In the blink of an eye
Realities can change
And, purpose adjusted
Flow with your tomorrow
In harmony with today.

"The creative and the emotional flow together as the universal energies create a new harmony within and ease the burdens of the day with a fresh rhythm to life itself. Rhythm should always be a focus, as it changes, lifts, and takes on a new pattern. Timing is everything. Pace yourself and allow the new energies to synchronize yours as you are pulled into a new dance of creation. Creative energies will be constantly flowing, so create channels for them to manifest within your realities. Take the time to play with those energies for they will help to bring greater abundance into your lives. Use the creative and apply it to those difficulties that have been bothering you; the more creative you are the richer the solutions. Blending with the creative is a joyful experience."

"Allow this energy to be manifest with fun and laughter; no one ever said solutions had to be serious and profound. The more laughter you bring into your lives, the greater the rewards. The emotions, as well, flow in harmony with creation. As you incorporate the creative into your lives, the emotional stretches and kinks are released, burdens crumble, and there is greater freedom on many different levels within you. Enjoy the time of fun and celebration for that aspect of the inner you is not always brought out when there are times of stress. The old adage that "laughter is the best medicine" is very true. Laughter and joy bring harmony and peace into your realities. No matter how difficult a situation if you can genuinely find laughter you break the spell of worry and find solutions that bring healing and abundance."

Sweet and Sour

That over which you have toiled
Bears fruit that is both sweet and sour
Ponder both extremes
For there is benefit in all.

"Always try to be focused upon letting go of issues the have become burdens carried for some time. Take time for forgiveness, not so much of others, but of the self for holding onto situations that no longer have import to our lives. Often we carry slights that become wounds, when not attended. Letting go of these issues will allow healing and growth to take place. It is not by accident that healing and growth are associated with the same color and chakra. By letting go of hurts and anger we free energy to be other directed towards growth and evolution of the spirit. Hanging onto anger or hurt weights us down and prevents us from ascension and growth, evolution and initiation to the grater dimensions that our spirits strive for."

"When put in this perspective much becomes petty and silly; after all who would want to be held back from the wondrous magical realms that are so close by petty slights or anger? Forgiveness is an inner emotion that once embraced shifts the outward expression of the soul energy. It changes your whole demeanor and how others perceive you. It does not happen overnight but once begun the process can be felt and movement seen. It starts on the conscious level and moves to the core of the spirit. It is a journey well worth the effort."

White Light

Out of time words gather form
A wisdom touched by the Infinite
The perspective of mankind shifts
And white light, through crystal,
Forms rainbows.
You provide some of the words
They must be released in order
To gather with those of others.

"Pay attention to what you need, what nurtures you, and what brings you joy. Life sometimes gets in the way of remembering that our focus has to me on the self in order for us to evolve and in turn help others. Some have gotten caught up in the theory that we must be totally dedicated to the service of others in order to be spiritual. The reality is that if we have not focused upon our own needs, if we have not taken the time to heal ourselves, we are of no good to others. On a spiritual level we do serve others as well as ourselves, but if the vessel that brings the energy is cracked and not cared for, we have nothing to bring to the table. This does not mean that it is all right to be selfish; it means that in order to be effective we must care for ourselves as well as sharing with others. You must focus upon the self and what you need to be vibrantly alive and joyful. Without those qualities your energy does not reach out to others. We heal and share only when those aspects have been addressed within us.
Take the time to nurture yourself, pamper yourself and the light and joy form that experience spills over to others and helps them to find their own inner lights and evolve into the healing process as well. Two excellent examples of this process are Mother Theresa and Gandhi. Look at their lives and what they were able to do … only after they had addressed their own issues and brought peace and joy to their own hearts."

Dead End

A dead end always can be fruitful
You need only the vision to go beyond.
That which others discard
You can turn into abundance.

"Try always to be embraced by a new flow of energy that opens us to greater freedom than ever before. Strive for expanded horizons and greater insight into the inner gifts we bring into this reality. You will then feel as if blockages have been removed and you are now free to move ahead on many projects that have been in a holding pattern for quiet a while. Feel a new breeze within the spirit that draws you forward into new endeavors and frees you from the ruts of the mundane. The openings have always been there it's just that your vision has cleared and you will see new channels and openings for your thoughts and dreams. Allow those dreams and thoughts to grow wings and release them into this new energy for when they take flight they soar to the upper limits and become reality. What you hold inside has to wait, what you release to the potential of the universe takes on a life of its own and draws you along in a new and magical dance of creation. Celebrate!"

On the Way to Eternity

As you flow through time
On your way to eternity
You plant seeds with all you touch
Nurture them with your love and light.
Your harvest is great
With abundance for all
And your garden reseeds itself
Sharing the fruit of love and answering a call.

"One draws into one's life no more than what is sent out to others. It is an elemental truth and a fact that all major and many minor religious beliefs are based upon; "As you sow so shall you reap". While everyone knows the statement, it is usually filed away with old wives tales. However, this cosmic law is clearly illustrated within their lives and many will be sent back to the drawing board to reconsider how they interact with their fellow man. It is a very important time for everyone and the awareness of the results of our actions and words will be more firmly imprinted upon our consciousness than ever before. All will be sent to rethink words and deeds, and many will change their approach to their realities. Those who often complain about how they are treated will be sent back to examine how they treat others."

Completed

The crystal light shakes free the dust
And casts out shadows that lingered long
The promise, free, now to be completed.

"Times of transition are often unsettling and sometimes even feared. There are those that fight change at every turn of the road and finally end up having to make great changes instead of many smaller ones. Transition, change; it's in the air and the energies swirl, fueled by these energies. The spirit is evolving into greater awareness and moving into new dimensions of understanding. There is much change going on within the energy of everyone. Some will dig in their heels and fight it, while others will embrace it and welcome the changes it brings. Transition means you can literally redefine yourself and move in new directions open yourself to the greater potentials the universe has for you. It is a time of growth and celebration. For those who choose to fight it and not grow, there will eventually be the feeling of isolation as others grow beyond them. For those who choose to flow with the energy and trust that the universe knows what it is doing there is expansion and new beginnings."

New Meaning

A call from the past
Opens a door to the future.
You acknowledge a part of yourself
And find Wholeness at last.
The core of the spark within you
Casts rainbows upon your soul,
Giving your vision crystal clarity
And new meaning.
You reach for greater awareness
Achieving more than ever imagined.
You touch not only yourself, but humanity as well
And become a part of all creation.

"It is a time for creating new foundations for the expanded awareness that is soon to become a part of our realities. It is a time of planting the seeds of creation, and a time when creative thoughts and plans will seem to tumble out at every opportunity. Gather them and nurture them, for they bring the potential of enriching you greatly if cared for. It is a time when foundations are laid that will support change and growth in the days and years to come. Make sure that when laying these foundations you are careful and meticulous for it is very important to attend to all of the details and finite issues now, so that what you build in the future does not crumble for lack of proper support. This refers to not only physical structures but to emotional ones as well, so use care as you build not only on the physical but emotional and intellectual planes as well. Caution and care taken now will provide a secure and stable platform for growth and expansion in the future. This is the time for insight and care so that at a later date you can be secure in the foundations that you have laid down."

Each Thought a Seed

A seed is planted in fertile soil
The seasons pass and sprouts it not.
A wanderer comes and pauses a while
He shares his wisdom and then moves on.

The words fall as rain upon the seed,
Caress it, spark it, and life reaches out.
Through fertile soil it bursts upon us.
A flower of wisdom without a doubt.

For all to see, for all to share
Each thought's a seed, each word a prayer.
Each flower of truth holds wisdom dear.
When the time is right the way is clear.

"When barriers have been lowered, there is a greater expanse of potential. Where there were areas when you saw no openings for growth, where there were no options or choices, where you felt claustrophobic, now, there is freedom to be yourself and express what is within you. There is suddenly freedom for growth and potentials seem limitless. A shadow has been withdrawn and the light now shines on all manner of choices and chances to expand your realities and consciousness. It is a time of freedom to be and become what you have dreamed of. The gates to the future are wide open and you are free to stretch yourself and to grow into the potential that has rested within for so long. Your vision for your future expands and the potentials are limitless. Allow yourselves to grow and reach for the stars; for that is indeed the legacy left to you by generations of your souls development. Freedom of spirit is yours and you need only claim it and embrace it for it to become an integral part of your reality."

Spiritual Stream

The crystal within flows and beckons
The reuniting with the soul's dream.
The colors swirl and become one
Within the light, that spiritual stream.

As energy changes and flows to the light
A dream is fulfilled, a shadow is banished.
You take up a charge, a question unanswered
The way is now clear, the blocks have all vanished.

"New energy flows throughout the hearts and minds of all mankind. There is a feeling of new direction and change, a greater awareness of the spiritual energies within us all and that just perhaps there is a way to achieve harmony and peace. This of course requires that all exercise free will and look toward the common good. This is a pathway, which will certainly be difficult, but not impossible. One not traveled before, and yet easily done once the first step is taken. It matters not how long it takes us, for we have all of eternity. What is important is that the first step be taken, and not by those in power but rather the common folk. For the power really rests within each individual spirit, not single ones who have been given power. It is the collective energies of the masses that will take the first step and the others, well; they will just have to follow."

A Lifetime Past

There comes a call from memories past
A picture out of time.
A dream awakened from deep within
A reason given rhyme.
A talent lost comes to the fore
Renewed, it is reborn.
A lifetime past, brought forth in space
Awakens to the morn

"Wisdom is brought from out of time, stored within for generations of the soul's evolution. Wisdoms are gathered lifetime, after lifetime like the pieces of a gigantic puzzle to be reassembled, only when all of the pieces have been gathered. Through a lifetime the puzzle is brought back to wholeness and new insights and levels and dimensions of wisdom are brought forward into the consciousness of mankind. Eons ago, before recorded time, humanity embraced these wisdoms and used them wisely for the healing and abundance of all. And then, there was a time of darkness, when the magic and miracles were lost to the memories and stored within until it was time to open those doors once more and to use those skills and understandings to restore the peace within the human heart and consciousness. The emergence of those wisdoms and their incorporation into reality will start slowly. Those who first draw upon them and remember their power will help others to do the same. It will take time but as there is the dawning of the memories once again. There is an ascension of consciousness and new pathways will be found that bring true magic into the realms of everyday life."

After Thoughts

It is the hope of any author that their message gets across, and that wisdom on some level is imparted to those who take the time to share their work. That is my intent and hope in this book. The words that have cascaded onto paper came from a place deep inside of me; one that holds, what I call "magic". That I have the opportunity to share my simple gifts with others is perhaps the greatest gift of all. I'm just like any of you who pick up this book, we all came from the same source and have access to the same talents and gifts inside. I have been blessed with a life that has enabled me to find channels inside and reach into the wisdoms that are stored there. We all have the same richness within, whether from lifetimes past (as I believe), or from genetic memory, as others do. It matters not how it got there or where it came from, all that really matters is that the answers are there for us, if we can just find the pathway to them. We all have within us the talent, gifts, and wisdoms that provide the answers to all our questions, and open to us who the creators are and our relationships to them.

We all quest, in our own ways and times. We all march to the rhythm of the cosmos and we all will, eventually, come to the same conclusion; we are a family, conceived in love, scattered across the cosmos. We journey for the wisdom to unite within that love that created us, so we can once more be one with creation and experience the unconditional love that is always available to all of us. The final frontier is not out into space, but rather within to find the magic stored there and the keys to the legacies instilled into us by our creators. I don't have all the answers; I'm still searching like all of you. What I do have is some insight into how to start to open some of those channels. I hope these words and rhymes give you pause to ponder and perhaps lead you to find your own personal magic.

Barbara DeLong

About The Author

Barbara DeLong is an internationally known radio podcast host, author, artist, poet, lecturer, ordained minister, and documentarian.
-        The Cosmic Deck of Initiation – this is a spiritual deck of hand painted mandala cards, which she painted, to be used for private divination and spiritual growth.
-        2011 Megalithomania conference documentary "Secrets of the Stones" - writer, narrator, co-producer with her late husband Patrick Cooke.
-        Her radio podcast, Night-Light Radio is intended to be just that in a time when many are awakening to the gifts and talents that they carry within. Her interviews with authors and gifted individuals help others to gain insight into themselves as well as the reality in which we dwell. She provides a platform for many to share the truths they have uncovered and the insights that can change our perception of the world in which we live.
-        Her website, Barbaradelong.com, is a teaching site combining personal information and a plethora of spiritual material.

Made in United States
Orlando, FL
29 March 2023